MW00356046

DLI PARENT BOOKS

SPEAKING TOGETHER™ in TAGALOG

Primary Level, Book 1

Let's talk about school.
Pag usapan natin ang eswkelahan.

Writer: **Marie Urquidi**

Illustrator: **Tracy Lynn Rabago**

Tagalog Editor: **William Tang**

WATCH VIDEOS TO HELP WITH PRONUNCIATION
www.DLIParentBooks.com

Dear Reader,

As you use DLI Parent Books, please keep in mind that the translations are reflective of the editor's use of the language. Different regions of the Philippines use different expressions, so the phrases selected for this book are casual and often referred to as Manila Tagalog.

Please use DLI Parent Books to encourage a love of learning a new language.

Thanks for choosing DLI Parent Books to encourage speaking Tagalog in your home.

Best,

Marie

Check out Videos
to hear some of the phrases
used in this book.
www.dliparentbooks.com

INTRODUCTION

Marie Tang Urquidi, Creator

As a mom of three living in Southern California, I was raised speaking only English. Both of my parents came from the Philippines, and like myself and my husband, many families of different cultures didn't pass on their native language to their children. I feel very fortunate to have my children in a Spanish Dual Language Immersion program where they will be taught to speak, read, and think in Spanish by the time they graduate. Their achievement in learning a new language has been amazing, but I frequently found myself unable to bring more Spanish dialogue into our home. Through our school's program, I learned that modeling the best linguistic pronunciation wasn't necessary for learning a new language. In fact, daily practice and consistency were more valuable for new language learners. I developed these books to bring language into our home and make it easier for parents to be part of their children's journey to becoming bilingual or even trilingual!

WHY DLI PARENT BOOKS?

1) EASY TO USE
I took a few Spanish classes in high school, so I thought I could easily communicate with my kindergartners. While working with them on their Spanish homework, I found that I was intimidated and realized I needed more encouragement. I created the scripted prompts and activities as a way to ease myself, parents, and children into speaking and learning a new language together.

2) COMPLIMENT WITH OTHER LANGUAGE PROGRAMS
With so many other language learning programs, books, and apps, I wanted DLI Parent Books to be another resource to accompany what is already available to them at home and at school. My goal was to create a product that allows users to casually converse with ease.

3) HERITAGE
I grew up with Tagalog spoken in the home. Though I never learned the language, I'm using DLI Parent Books to introduce Tagalog to my children. I feel it'll help connect them to their Filipino heritage and gain more quality time with their grandparents. I'm happy to report that I've even learned some Tagalog since I began this project.

4) MADE FOR TALKING!
These books intend to help adults and children speak, listen, and learn a new language by doing a page or more a day. Through these easy activities, the goal is to make it fun and engaging for daily use.

5) LIFE-LONG BENEFITS
There are many benefits to being multi-lingual. Beyond having an academic advantage, a bilingual student will have more career and cultural opportunities later in life. Our family has focused on making sure our children have a bright and fulfilling future. These books not only create more quality time for us, but it encourages our children to learn more about themselves and the people around them.

HOW TO USE THIS BOOK

1) Gather **CRAYONS and PENCILS** for this workbook.

2) SIT ON THE LEFT SIDE of your student, so that you can read the ADULT PROMPTS more easily.

3) Review **page 2** for **ADULT PHRASES AND STUDENT PHRASES**. You will begin to use these phrases frequently as you go through the book.

To listen and repeat some of the phrases used in this book, go to: **DLIParentBooks.com/Videos**

4) Pick any activity you'd like to do and always **START AT THE TOP OF THE ACTIVITY PAGE** so that the child always focuses on the page in front of them. Use the Left Page to begin a conversation with your child.

5) Aim for ONE OR TWO ACTIVITIES PER DAY.

Right Side: ACTIVITY PAGE FOR THE STUDENT

Left Side: CONVERSATION PROMPTS FOR THE ADULT

STUDENT PHRASES

When speaking to elders, add "po" to be respectful.

Yes -Oo. / Opo.
(oh-oh / oh-poh)

No -Hindi. / Hindi po.
(heen-dih / heen-dih poh)

I don't know. **-Hindi ko (po) alam.**
(heen-dih koh ah-lahm)

I don't understand. **-Hindi ko (po) maintindihan.**
(heen-dih koh mah-een-teen-dee-hahn)

Can you help me? **-Maari mo (po) ba akong tulungan.**
(mah-ah-ree moh bah ah-kohng too-loo-NGAn)

How do you say _____ in Tagalog?
Paano mo (po) sabihin ang _____ sa Tagalog?
(pah-ah-noh moh sah-bee-heen ahng _____ sah tah-gah-lohg)

Thank you. **-Salamat (po).** *(sah-lah-maht)*

I'm learning to speak Tagalog.
Nagaaral akong magsalita ng tagalog.
(nahg-ah-ahr-ahl ah-kohng mahg-sah-lee-tah nang tah-gah-lohg)

This is fun. **-Ito (po) ay masaya**
(ee-toh eye mah-sah-yah)

Can we do a Maze?
Maaari (po) ba tayong gumawa ng maze?
(mah-ah-ahree bah tah-yong goo-mah-wah nang maze)

Let me try. **-Hayaan mong subukan ko (po).**
(hah-yah-ahn mohng soo-boo-kahn koh)

BASICS OF TAGALOG PRONUNCIATION

Tagalog is a phonetic language that is quite easy to pronounce, but there are some main sounds that differ from the way they are pronounced in English. To help with the challenge of speaking Tagalog, try repeating the new sounds and speaking at an average conversation level. Your mouth will learn to produce these sounds correctly.

Pronuncation is important. The english word "contest" can have 2 different meanings depending on where you stress the word.
CON-test - competition and **con-TEST - to oppose**
In Tagalog, "baon" can also have two different meanings.
BA-on - supply or allowance and **ba-ON - buried**

Vowels:
A (ah) : "a" sounds the same as the one contained in the word "f<u>a</u>ther"
E (eh): "e" sounds the same as "g<u>e</u>t".
I (ee): "i" is pronounced in the same way as in "mach<u>i</u>ne".
O (oh): "o" sounds the same way as in "<u>o</u>pen".
U (oo): "u" has the same pronunciation as "sp<u>oo</u>n".

"NG":
NG: NG is the 12th letter of the Abakada and is pronounced "<u>nung</u>."
Ng: When "ng" is used in a sentence it mean "of" and is prounounced "<u>nang</u>."
An example, "anak <u>ng</u> babae" translates to "a woman's child."
Nga: The sound "nga" can be easily sounded out when you say "sing along." When you say it fast, you get the sound for "nga" in "si**nga**long."

"MGA": Pronounced "<u>mung-ah.</u>"
When "mga" is used before nouns, it turns the word/noun plural. For example, animal is "hayop." The word "animals" requires adding "mga," so it would be "mga hayop."

ALPHABET: Learn the ABAKADA starting on page 24. There are English words that are not part of the Abakada. For example, the letter "J" does not exist, but the sound does appear in some Tagalog words. For example, "diyan" means "there." The pronunciation of "diyan" is "john."

RESOURCES: Go to DLIParentBooks.com for a video tutorial on pronunciation of the phrases you will be saying in this book.

LET'S COLOR TOGETHER

Sama sama nating kulayan

sah-mah sah-mah
nah-tihng koo-la-yahn

TALKING AND COLORING

READ PHRASES THAT ARE APPLICABLE TO YOU

I am your mom.   **-Ako ang nanay mo.**

(ah-koh ahng nah-nye moh)

I am your dad.   **-Ako ang tatay mo.**

(ah-koh ahng tah-tie moh)

Grandma   **-Lola** (loh-lah)

Grandpa   **-Lolo** (loh-loh)

BE PLAYFUL

Guess what I am.   **-Hulaan mo kung ano ako.**

.   (hoo-lah-ahn moh koong ah-noh ah-koh)

I am a plane.   **-Ako ay eroplano.** (ah-koh eye eh-roh-plah-noh)

I am a monkey.   **-Ako ay unggoy.** (ah-koh eye oong-goy)

What do you want to be?   **-Ano ang gusto mo maging?**

(ah-noh ahng gooh-stoh moh mah-geeng)

Pretend.   **-Magkunwari.** (mahg-koon-wah-ree)

A ninja.   **-Ninja.** (neen-jah) - do some ninja moves

A dog.   **-Aso.** (ah-soh) - bark like a dog

A cat.   **-Pusa.** (pooh-sah) - meow like a cat

PHRASES FOR COLORING

Let's Color.   **-Mag kulay tayo.** (mahg koo-lie tah-yoh)

Which color do you   **-Alin kulay ang gusto mong gamitin?**

want to use?   (ah-leen koo-lie ahng goos-toh mohng gah-mee-tihn)

Red -**Pula** (poo-lah)   Blue -**Bughaw** (boog-how)

Yellow -**Dilaw** (dee-lao)   Brown -**Kayumanggi** (kah-yoo-mahng-gee)

Green -**Verde** (behr-deh)   Orange -**Kahel** (kah-hel)

I am a doctor.
Ako ay isang doktor.
(ah-koh eye ee-sahng dohk-tohr)

TALKING AND COLORING

READ PHRASES THAT ARE APPLICABLE TO YOU

You are a boy.   **-Ikaw ay isang batang lalaki.**

(ee-kaow aye ee-sahng bah-tahng lah-lah-kee)

You are a girl.   **-Ikaw ay isang batang babae.**

(ee-kaow aye ee-sahng bah-tahng bah-ba-eh)

You are bright.   **-Ikaw ay matalino.** *(ee-kaow aye mah-tah-lee-noh)*

You are nice.   **-Ikaw ay mabait.** *(ee-kaow aye mah-bah-eet)*

You are a great kid.   **-Ikaw ay magaling na bata.**

(ee-kaow aye mah-gah-leeng nah bah-tah)

DRAW ON THE NEXT PAGE AND USE TAGALOG PHRASES BELOW

This is your head.   **-Ito ang iyong ulo.** *(ee-toh ahng ee-yohng ooh-loh)*

This is your body.   **-Ito ang iyong katawan.** *(ee-toh ahng ee-yohng kah-tah-wahn)*

I'm going to draw   **-Susunod kong iguguhit ang iyong mga braso.**

   your arms next.   *(soo-soo-nohd kohng ee-goo-goo-hit ahng*

ee-yohng mung-ah brah-soh)

Here are your legs.   **-Ito ang iyong mga binti.**

(ee-toh ahng ee-yohng mung-ah been-tih)

What do you think?   **-Ano sa palagay mo?** *(ah-noh sah pah-lah-guy moh)*

Now it's your turn   **-Ngayon ikaw na ang mag guguhit.**

   to draw.   *(NGA-yohn ee-kaow nah ahng mahg goo-goo-hiht)*

Draw your eyes.   **-Iguhit ang iyong mga mata.**

(ee-goo-hit ahng ee-yohng mung-ah mah-tah)

Draw your nose.   **-Iguhit ang iyong ilong.** *(ee-goo-hit ahng ee-yong ee-long)*

Draw your mouth.   **-Iguhit ang iyong bibig.** *(ee-goo-hit ahng ee-yong bee-big)*

Draw your hair.   **-Iguhit ang iyong buhok.** *(ee-goo-hit ahng ee-yohng boo-hohk)*

Good job.   **-Ayos.** *(ah-yoos)*

I'm going to draw you.
Iguguhit kita.
(ee-goo-goo-hit kee-tah)

TALKING AND COLORING

USE THE PHRASES BELOW TO COLOR THE NEXT PAGE

This is a small turtle.   **-Ito ay isang maliit na pagong.**

(ee-toh eye ee-sahng mah-lee-it nah pah-gong)

What should we color it?   **-Ano ang dapat nating ikulay?**

(ah-noh ahng dah-paht nah-teeng ee-koo-lye)

This is a purple crayon.   **-Ito ay isang krayolang lila.**

(ee-toh eye ee-sahng kray-oh-lahng lee-lah)

Which color do you   **-Aling kulay ang nais mong gamitin?**

want to use?   *(ah-ling koo-lay ahng nah-ees mohng gah-mee-teen)*

Red -**Pula** *(pooh-lah)*   Blue -**Bughaw** *(boog-how)*

Yellow -**Dilaw** *(dee-lao)*   Brown -**Kayumanggi** *(kah-yoo-mahng-gee)*

Green -**Berde** *(behr-deh)*   Orange -**Kahel** *(kah-hel)*

That's a good idea!   **-Magandang ideya iyan!**

(mah-gahn-dahng ee-deh-yah ee-yan)

This is the turtle's shell.   **-Ito ang talukab ng pagong.**

(ee-toh ahng tah-loo-kahb nang pah-gohng)

Do you want to name   **-Nais mo bang pangalanan ang pagong na ito?**

this turtle?   *(nah-ees moh bahng pah-NGA-lah-nahn ahng*

pah-gong nah ee-toh)

Yes   **-Oo.** *(oh-oh)*

What do you want to   **-Ano ang gusto mong ipangalan sa pagong mo?**

name your tutrle?   *(ah-noh ahng goo-stoh mohg ee-pah-NGA-lahn sah*

pah-gohng moh)

Let me write the name.   **-Hayaan mong isulat ko ang pangalan.**

(ha-yah-ahn mohng ee-soo-laht koh ahng

pahng-ah-lahn)

This is a small turtle.
Ito ay isang maliit na pagong.

(ee-toh aye ee-sahng mah-lee-it nah pah-gong)

Name / **Pangalan** *(pang-NGA-lahn)* : _____

TALKING AND COLORING

USE PHRASES THAT ARE APPLICABLE TO YOU

This is a jump rope.   **-Ito ay luksong-lubid.**

(ee-toh eye look-sohng loo-bid)

Can you jump rope?   **-Kaya mo bang mag luksong lubid?**

(kah-yah moh bahng mahg look-song loo-bid)

Is it easy?   **-Madali ba?** *(mah-dah-lee bah)*

Is it hard?   **-Mahirap ba?** *(mah-hee-rahp bah)*

Do you want to learn?   **-Gusto mong matuto?** *(goo-stoh mohng mah-too-toh)*

Let's stand up.   **-Tumayo tayo.**

(too-mah-yoh tah-yoh)

Let's pretend to run.   **-Magpanggap tayong tumatakbo?**

(mahg-pahng-gahp tah-yohng too-mah-tahk-boh)

Pretend to run faster.   **-Magpanggap tayong tumakbo nang mas mabilis.**

(mahg-pahng-gahp tah-yohng too-mah-tahk-boh

nahng mahs mah-bee-lees)

Pretend to run in slow motion. **-Magpanggap tayong tumakbo ng mabagal.**

(mahg-pahng-gahp tah-yohng too-mahk-boh

nang mah-bah-gahl)

PHRASES FOR COLORING

Let's Color. **-Mag kulay tayo.** *(mahg koo-lie tah-yoh)*

Which color do you want to use? **-Alin kulay gusto mong gamitin?**

(ah-leen koo-lie goos-toh mohng gah-mee-teen)

Red -**Pula** *(poo-lah)*   Blue -**Bughaw** *(boog-how)*

Yellow -**Dilaw** *(dee-lao)*   Brown -**Kayumanggi** *(kah-yoo-mahng-gee)*

Green -**Berde** *(behr-deh)*   Orange -**Kahel** *(kah-hel)*

Jump Rope
Luksong Lubid
(look-song loo-bid)

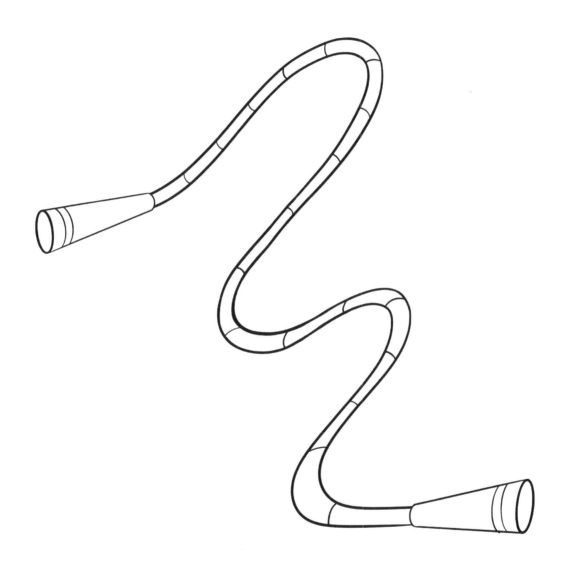

TALKING AND COLORING

DESCRIBE THINGS IN THE ROOM THAT ARE FAR FROM YOU

Let's describe things in the room that are far from us. **-I larawan natin ang mga bagay sa silid na malayo sa atin.** *(ee lah-rah-wan nah-tin ahng mah-NGA bah-guy sah sih-lid nah mah-lah-yo sah ah-tin)*

What do you see? **-Ano ang nakita mo?** *(ah-noh ahng nah-kee-tah moh)*

That is a picture. **-Yan ay larawan.** *(yahn eye lah-rah-wahn)*

That is a cup. **-Yan ay tasa.** *(yahn eye tah-sah)*

That is a TV. **-Yan an tv.** *(yahn eye tee-bee)*

That is a couch. **-Yan ay sopa.** *(yahn eye soh-pah)*

That is a refrigerator. **-Yan ay refrigerator.** *(yahn eye refrigerator)*

That is a rug. **-Yan ay basahan.** *(yahn eye bah-sah-hahn)*

That's the door. **-Yan ay pintuan.** *(yahn eye peen-too-ahn)*

PHRASES FOR COLORING

Let's Color. **-Mag kulay tayo.**

(mahg koo-lie tah-yoh)

Which color do you want to use? **-Alin kulay gusto mong gamitin?**

(ah-leen koo-lie goos-toh mohng gah-mee-teen)

Red -**Pula** *(poo-lah)*   Blue -**Bughaw** *(boog-how)*

Yellow -**Dilaw** *(dee-lao)*   Brown -**Kayumanggi** *(kah-yoo-mahng-gee)*

Green -**Berde** *(behr-deh)*   Orange -**Kahel** *(kah-hel)*

Purple -**Lila / Ube** *(lee-lah / oo-beh)*   Pink -**Rosas** *(roh-sahs)*

Black -**Itim** *(ee-teem)*   White -**Puti** *(pooh-tee)*

Bird
Ibon
(ee-bohn)

TALKING AND COLORING

USE PHRASES THAT ARE APPLICABLE TO YOU

Let's see what we
have around here.

-Tingnan natin kung ano ang mayroon tayo dito.

(teeng-nahn nah-teen kuhng ah-noh ahng

my-roh-on tah-yoh dee-toh)

We have crayons on the table. **-Mayroon kaming mga krayola sa mesa.**

(my-roh-on kah-meeng mah-NGA krah-yoh-lah

sah meh-sah)

We have a crayon on the table **-Mayroon kaming krayola sa mesa.**

(my-roh-on kah-meeng krah-yoh-lah sah meh-sah)

We have pencils, crayons,
and markers.

-Mayroon kaming mga lapis, krayola, at mga marker.

(my-roh-on kah-meeng mah-NGA lah-pees,

krah-yoh-lah, aht mah-NGA mahr-kehr)

We have our workbook. **-Mayroon kaming workbook.**

(my-roh-on kah-meeng workbook)

We have an eraser. **-Mayroon kaming pambura.**

(my-roh-on kah-meeng pahm-boo-rah)

We have water on the table. **-Mayroon kaming tubig sa mesa.**

(my-roh-on kah-meeng too-big sah meh-sah)

PHRASES FOR COLORING

Let's Color. **-Mag kulay tayo.** *(mahg koo-lie tah-yoh)*

Which color do you want to use? **-Alin kulay ang gusto mong gamitin?**

(ah-leen koo-lie ahng goos-toh mohng gah-mee-teen)

Red -**Pula** *(poo-lah)*   Blue -**Bughaw** *(boog-how)*

Yellow -**Dilaw** *(dee-lao)*   Brown -**Kayumanggi** *(kah-yoo-mahng-gee)*

Green -**Berde** *(behr-deh)*   Orange -**Kahel** *(kah-hel)*

Purple -**Lila / Ube***(lee-lah / oo-beh)* Pink -**Rosas** *(roh-sahs)*

Tickets
Mga Tiket
(mah-NGA tee-keht)

TALKING AND COLORING

USE PHRASES THAT ARE APPLICABLE TO YOU

What else can you put
in your backpack?

-**Ano pa ang mailalagay mo sa iyong backpack?**
(ah-noh pah ahng mah-ee-lah--lah-guy moh sah ee-yohng backpack)

Lunch.

-**Tanghalian.** *(tahng-hah-lee-ahn)*

Snack.

-**Meryenda.** *(mehr-yehn-dah)*

Water bottle.

-**Bote ng tubig.**
(boh-teh nung too-big)

What can fit into my pocket?

-**Ano ang maaaring magkasya sa aking bulsa?**
(ah-noh ahng mah-ah-ah-reeng mahg-kah-syhah sah ah-keeng bool-sah)

Keys.

-**Mga susi.**
(mung-ah soo-see)

What goes in your shoe?

-**Ano ang pumasok sa sapatos mo?**
(ah-noh ahng pooh-mah-sohk sah sah-pah-tohs moh)

Your foot.

-**Ang iyong paa.** *(ahng ee-yohng pah-ah)*

What goes in your cereal?

-**Ano ang sangkap sa iyong cereal?**
(ah-noh ahng sahng-kahp sah ee-yohng see-ree-ahl)

Milk.

-**Gatas.** *(gah-tahs)*

PHRASES FOR COLORING

Let's Color. -**Mag kulay tayo.** *(mahg koo-lie tah-yoh)*

Which color do you want to use? -**Alin kulay ang gusto mong gamitin?**
(ah-leen koo-lie ahng goos-toh mohng gah-mee-teen)

Red -**Pula** *(poo-lah)*   Blue -**Bughaw** *(boog-how)*

Yellow -**Dilaw** *(dee-lao)*   Brown -**Kayumanggi** *(kah-yoo-mahng-gee)*

Green -**Berde** *(behr-deh)*   Orange -**Kahel** *(kah-hel)*

Purple -**Lila / Ube** *(lee-lah / oo-beh)*   Pink -**Rosas** *(roh-sahs)*

Black -**Itim** *(ee-teem)*   White -**Puti** *(pooh-tee)*

My jacket is in my backpack.
Nasa backpack ko ang aking jacket.
(nah-sah backpack koh ahng ah-keeng djah-keht)

ABAKADA ALPHABET

The Filipino alphabet has undergone several editions leading to its modernization. The pages you will see are the original ABAKADA letters with its pronunciation, which will help you read Tagalog more efficiently. Today, many students in the Philippines read the alphabet using the English pronunciation.

Here is a little history:

During the Commonwealth Era, the Philippines realized the need to adopt one national language, and they decided on Tagalog. The government created an official dictionary and grammar book for the new national language.

In 1940, Lope K. Santos introduced the Abakada alphabet (named after its first four letters), comprising of 20 letters. This created a local writing system for the Tagalog language. Santos ensured that one letter is read in one specific sound. For instance, since C, Q, and K sound the same in Tagalog, only one should be retained. This trimmed the Spanish-based 32-letter abecedario to 20 letters.

By 1976, majority of Filipinos still embraced the other native Philippine languages. This caused debates regarding the definition of having a national language. Tagalog was then renamed as Filipino and undergone more development. Eleven letters came back – C, CH, F, J, LL, Ñ, Q, RR, V, X, and Z – covering the other Filipino languages still using them.

In 1987, the present 28-letter Filipino alphabet was finally established, 20 abakada letters remained; so do the letters C, F, J, Ñ , Q, V, X, Z since they're used in many regional languages; but the letters CH, LL, and RR were dropped. In a nutshell, language scholars brainstormed, and the rest is history.

LET'S WRITE TOGETHER

Sabay tayong magsulat

sah-bye tah-yohng mahg-soo-laht

ABAKADA ALPHABET

Aa (ah)

Ba (*bah*)

Ka (*kah*)

Da (dah)

Ee (eh)

Ga (*gah*)

Ha (*hah*)

Ii (ee)

La (*lah*)

Ma (*mah*)

Na (*nah*)

ABAKADA ALPHABET

Nga (NGA)
Oo (oh)
Pa (*pah*)
Ra (*rah*)
Sa (*sah*)
Ta (*tah*)
Uu (ooh)
Wa (*wah*)
Ya (*yah*)

SPANISH ALPHABET

Notice the vowel sounds are the same for Abakada.

Aa (a) - *AH*

Bb (be) - *BAY*

Cc (ce) - *SAY*

Dd (de) - *DAY*

Ee (e) - *EY*

Ff (efe) - *EH-FAY*

Gg (ge) - *HAY*

Hh (hache) *AH-CHAY*

Ii (i) - *EE*

Jj (jota) - *HOH-TAH*

Kk (kah) - *KAH*

Ll (ele) - *EH-LAY*

Nn (ene) - *EH-NEH*

Ññ (eñe) - *EH-NYAY*

Oo (o) - *OH*

Pp (pe) - *PAY*

Qq (cu) - *KOO*

Rr (erre) - *EH-RRAY*

Ss (ese) - *EH-SAY*

Tt (te) - *TAY*

Uu (u) - *OOH*

Vv (uve) - *OOH-VEY*

Ww (doble uve)

DOH-BLAY OOH-VEH

Xx (equis) - *EH-KEES*

Yy (ye) - *YEH*

Zz (zeta) - *SEH-TAH*

Aa (ah)

I'm going to write the letter A. **-Isusulat ko ang letra A.**
(ee-soo-soo-laht koh ahng lehtra ah)

Trace the letter. **-Bakasin ang letra.** *(bah-kah-seen ahng leh-trah)*

Now you try. **-Ikaw naman ang sumubok.** *(ee-kaw nah-mahn ahng soo-moh-bohk)*

Practice writing. **-Pagsasanay sa pagsulat.** *(pahg-sah-sah-nye sah pahg-soo-laht)*

Good job. **-Magaling.** *(mahg-ah-leeng)*

How do you say _____ in Tagalog?
Paano mo sabihin ang ____ sa Tagalog?
(pah-ah-noh moh sah-bee-heen ahng ____ sah tah-gah-lohg)

Aba *(ah-bah)* - Wow!

Abakada *(ah-bah-kah-dah)* - Alphabet

Abentura *(ah-ben-too-rah)* - Adventure

Artist *(ahr-teest)* - Artist

Ada *(ah-dah)* - Fairy

Agahan *(ah-ga-hahn)* - Breakfast

Agosto *(ah-gohs-toh)* - August

Araw *(ah-rao)* - Sun

Bb (bah)

I'm going to write the letter B -**Isusulat ko ang letra B.**
(ee-soo-soo-laht koh ahng lehtra bah)

Trace the letter. -**Bakasin ang letra.** *(bah-kah-seen ahng leh-trah)*

Now you try. -**Ikaw naman ang sumubok.** *(ee-kaw nah-mahn ahng soo-moh-bohk)*

Practice writing. -**Pagsasanay sa pagsulat.** *(pahg-sah-sah-nye sah pahg-soo-laht)*

Good job. -**Magaling.** *(mahg-ah-leeng)*

How do you say _____ in Tagalog?
Paano mo sabihin ang ____ sa Tagalog?
(pah-ah-noh moh sah-bee-heen ahng ____ sah tah-gah-lohg)

Baboy *(bah-boy)* - Pig

Bago *(bahg-oh)* - New

Baka *(bahk-ah)* - Cow

Bakasyon *(bah-kah-syohn)* - Vacation

Bakit *(bah-kit)* - Why

Bahay *(bah-hye)* - House

Babae *(bah-bah-eh)* - Lady/Female

Bagyo *(bahg-yoh)* - Storm

Baho *(bah-hoh)* - Bad Smell

Kk (kah)

I'm going to write the letter K **-Isusulat ko ang letra K.**
(ee-soo-soo-laht koh ahng lehtra kah)

Trace the letter. **-Bakasin ang letra.** *(bah-kah-seen ahng leh-trah)*

Now you try. **-Ikaw naman ang sumubok.** *(ee-kaw nah-mahn ahng soo-moh-bohk)*

Practice writing. **-Pagsasanay sa pagsulat.** *(pahg-sah-sah-nye sah pahg-soo-laht)*

Good job. **-Magaling.** *(mahg-ah-leeng)*

How do you say _____ in Tagalog?
Paano mo sabihin ang ____ sa Tagalog?
(pah-ah-noh moh sah-bee-heen ahng ____ sah tah-gah-lohg)

Kaibigan *(kahy-bee-guhn)* - Friend

Kabayo *(kah-bye-yoh)* - Horse

Kuya *(koo-yah)* - Older Brother

Kabiglaanan *(kah-beeg-lah-ahn-ahn)* - To be surprised

Kotse *(koh-che)* - Car

Kulay *(kooh-lye)* - Color

Kalendaryo *(kah-lehn-dah-ryoh)* - Calendar

Kama *(kah-MAH)* - Bed

Dd (dah)

I'm going to write the letter D. **-Isusulat ko ang letra D.**
(ee-soo-soo-laht koh ahng lehtra dah)

Trace the letter. **-Bakasin ang letra.** *(bah-kah-seen ahng leh-trah)*

Now you try. **-Ikaw naman ang sumubok.** *(ee-kaw nah-mahn ahng soo-moh-bohk)*

Practice writing. **-Pagsasanay sa pagsulat.** *(pahg-sah-sah-nye sah pahg-soo-laht)*

Good job. **-Magaling.** *(mahg-ah-leeng)*

How do you say _____ in Tagalog?
Paano mo sabihin ang _____ sa Tagalog?
(pah-ah-noh moh sah-bee-heen ahng _____ sah tah-gah-lohg)

Daga *(dah-gah)* - Mouse

Dagat *(dah-gaht)* - Ocean

Daliri *(dah-lee-ree)* - Finger

Dalawa *(dah-lah-wah)* - Two

Disyembre *(dis-yehm-breh)* - December

Dilaw *(dee-laow)* - Yellow

Dito *(dee-toh)* - Here

Dalawampu *(dah-lah-wahm-pooh)* - Twenty

Ee (eh)

I'm going to write the letter E. **-Isusulat ko ang letra E.**
(ee-soo-soo-laht koh ahng lehtra eh)

Trace the letter. **-Bakasin ang letra.** *(bah-kah-seen ahng leh-trah)*

Now you try. **-Ikaw naman ang sumubok.** *(ee-kaw nah-mahn ahng soo-moh-bohk)*

Practice writing. **-Pagsasanay sa pagsulat.** *(pahg-sah-sah-nye sah pahg-soo-laht)*

Good job. **-Magaling.** *(mahg-ah-leeng)*

How do you say _____ in Tagalog?
Paano mo sabihin ang _____ sa Tagalog?
(pah-ah-noh moh sah-bee-heen ahng _____ sah tah-gah-lohg)

Ehemplo *(eh-hem-ploh)* - Example

Eksplorer *(eks-plohr-er)* - Explorer

Elepante *(eh-leh-pahn-teh)* - Elephant

Ensalada *(ehn-sah-lah-dah)* - Salad

Eskwela *(ehs-kweh-lah)* - School

Enero *(eh-neh-roh)* - January

Eroplano *(eh-roh-pla-noh)* - Airplane

Gg (gah)

I'm going to write the letter G. **-Isusulat ko ang letra G.**
(ee-soo-soo-laht koh ahng lehtra gah)

Trace the letter. **-Bakasin ang letra.** *(bah-kah-seen ahng leh-trah)*

Now you try. **-Ikaw naman ang sumubok.** *(ee-kaw nah-mahn ahng soo-moh-bohk)*

Practice writing. **-Pagsasanay sa pagsulat.** *(pahg-sah-sah-nye sah pahg-soo-laht)*

Good job. **-Magaling.** *(mahg-ah-leeng)*

How do you say _____ in Tagalog?
Paano mo sabihin ang ____ sa Tagalog?
(pah-ah-noh moh sah-bee-heen ahng ____ sah tah-gah-lohg)

Gabi *(gah-bee)* - Night

Gagamba *(gah-gahm-bah)* - Spider

Galamgam *(gah-lahm-gahm)* - To Tickle

Gatas *(gah-tahs)* - Milk

Gubat *(goo-baht)* - Forest

Gansa *(gahn-sah)* - Goose

Guwapo *(goo-wah-poh)* - Handsome

Garahe *(gah-rah-heh)* - Garage

Hh (ha)

I'm going to write the letter H -**Isusulat ko ang letra H.**
(ee-soo-soo-laht koh ahng lehtra ha)

Trace the letter. -**Bakasin ang letra.** *(bah-kah-seen ahng leh-trah)*

Now you try. -**Ikaw naman ang sumubok.** *(ee-kaw nah-mahn ahng soo-moh-bohk)*

Practice writing. -**Pagsasanay sa pagsulat.** *(pahg-sah-sah-nye sah pahg-soo-laht)*

Good job. -**Magaling.** *(mahg-ah-leeng)*

How do you say _____ in Tagalog?
Paano mo sabihin ang ____ sa Tagalog?
(pah-ah-noh moh sah-bee-heen ahng ____ sah tah-gah-lohg)

Hunyo *(hoon-yoh)* - June

Hulyo *(hool-yoh)* - July

Hardin *(hahr-deen)* - Garden

Hayop *(hah-yohp)* - Animal

Hindi *(heen-dee)* - No

Hinto *(heen-toh)* - Stops

Hala! *(hah-lah)* - Go ahead!

Halik *(hah-leek)* - Kiss

Hintay *(heen-tye)* - Wait

Ii (ee)

I'm going to write the letter I -**Isusulat ko ang letra I.**
(ee-soo-soo-laht koh ahng lehtra ee)

Trace the letter. -**Bakasin ang letra.** *(bah-kah-seen ahng leh-trah)*

Now you try. -**Ikaw naman ang sumubok.** *(ee-kaw nah-mahn ahng soo-moh-bohk)*

Practice writing. -**Pagsasanay sa pagsulat.** *(pahg-sah-sah-nye sah pahg-soo-laht)*

Good job. -**Magaling.** *(mahg-ah-leeng)*

How do you say _____ in Tagalog?
Paano mo sabihin ang ____ sa Tagalog?
(pah-ah-noh moh sah-bee-heen ahng ____ sah tah-gah-lohg)

Ibon *(ee-bohn)* - Bird

Isda *(ees-dah)* - Fish

Isa *(ee-sah)* - One

Itim *(ee-teem)* - Black

Ilog *(ee-lohg)* - River

Inom *(ee-nohm)* - Drink

Ina *(ee-nah)* - Mother

Itay *(ee-tye)* - Father

Ll (lah)

I'm going to write the letter L. **-Isusulat ko ang letra L.**
(ee-soo-soo-laht koh ahng lehtra lah)

Trace the letter. **-Bakasin ang letra.** *(bah-kah-seen ahng leh-trah)*

Now you try. **-Ikaw naman ang sumubok.** *(ee-kaw nah-mahn ahng soo-moh-bohk)*

Practice writing. **-Pagsasanay sa pagsulat.** *(pahg-sah-sah-nye sah pahg-soo-laht)*

Good job. **-Magaling.** *(mahg-ah-leeng)*

How do you say _____ in Tagalog?
Paano mo sabihin ang _____ sa Tagalog?
(pah-ah-noh moh sah-bee-heen ahng _____ sah tah-gah-lohg)

Lalaki *(lah-lah-kee)* - Man

Lunes *(looh-nehs)* - Monday

Linggo *(leeng-goh)* - Sunday

Lima *(lee-mah)* - Five

Labing-isa *(lah-beeng ee-sah)* - Eleven

Lila *(lee-lah)* - Purple

Lapis *(lah-pees)* - Pencil

Libro *(lee-broh)* - Book

Mm (mah)

I'm going to write the letter M. **-Isusulat ko ang letra M.**
(ee-soo-soo-laht koh ahng lehtra mah)

Trace the letter. **-Bakasin ang letra.** *(bah-kah-seen ahng leh-trah)*

Now you try. **-Ikaw naman ang sumubok.** *(ee-kaw nah-mahn ahng soo-moh-bohk)*

Practice writing. **-Pagsasanay sa pagsulat.** *(pahg-sah-sah-nye sah pahg-soo-laht)*

Good job. **-Magaling.** *(mahg-ah-leeng)*

How do you say _____ in Tagalog?
Paano mo sabihin ang _____ sa Tagalog?
(pah-ah-noh moh sah-bee-heen ahng _____ sah tah-gah-lohg)

Martes *(mahr-tehs)* - Tuesday

Maaraw *(mah-ahr-aow)* - Sunny

Miyerkoles *(mee-yehr-koh-lehs)* - Wednesday

Mainit *(mah-een-it)* - Hot

Maginaw *(mahg-ee-naw)* - Cold

Marso *(mahr-soh)* - March

Maganda *(mah-gahn-dah)* - Beautiful

Matulungin *(mah-too-loon-geen)* - Helpful

Nn (nah)

I'm going to write the letter N. **-Isusulat ko ang letra N.**
(ee-soo-soo-laht koh ahng lehtra nah)

Trace the letter. **-Bakasin ang letra.** *(bah-kah-seen ahng leh-trah)*

Now you try. **-Ikaw naman ang sumubok.** *(ee-kaw nah-mahn ahng soo-moh-bohk)*

Practice writing. **-Pagsasanay sa pagsulat.** *(pahg-sah-sah-nye sah pahg-soo-laht)*

Good job. **-Magaling.** *(mahg-ah-leeng)*

How do you say _____ in Tagalog?
Paano mo sabihin ang _____ sa Tagalog?
(pah-ah-noh moh sah-bee-heen ahng _____ sah tah-gah-lohg)

Nobyembre *(noh-beh-yehm-breh)* - November

Nabubusog *(nah-boo-boo-sohg)* - To be full

Nag-anyaya *(nahg-ahn-yah-yah)* - To invite

Nag-aaral *(nahg-ah-ahr-ahl)* - To study

Nag-abang *(nahg-ahb-ang)* - To wait for

Naniwala *(nah-nee-wah-lah)* - To believe

Nag-agahan *(nahg-ahg-ah-ahn)* - To eat breakfast

Ng ng (NGA)

I'm going to write the letter Ng. **-Isusulat ko ang letra Ng.**
(ee-soo-soo-laht koh ahng lehtra nung)

Trace the letter. **-Bakasin ang letra.** *(bah-kah-seen ahng leh-trah)*

Now you try. **-Ikaw naman ang sumubok.** *(ee-kaw nah-mahn ahng soo-moh-bohk)*

Practice writing. **-Pagsasanay sa pagsulat.** *(pahg-sah-sah-nye sah pahg-soo-laht)*

Good job. **-Magaling.** *(mahg-ah-leeng)*

How do you say _____ in Tagalog?
Paano mo sabihin ang _____ sa Tagalog?
(pah-ah-noh moh sah-bee-heen ahng _____ sah tah-gah-lohg)

Ngayon *(NGAA-yohn)* - Now

Ngiti *(NGEE-tih)* - Smile

Ngipin *(NGI-pihn)* - Teeth

Ngunit *(NGU-niht)* - But; However

Oo (oh)

I'm going to write the letter O. **-Isusulat ko ang letra O.**
(ee-soo-soo-laht koh ahng lehtra oh)

Trace the letter. **-Bakasin ang letra.** *(bah-kah-seen ahng leh-trah)*

Now you try. **-Ikaw naman ang sumubok.** *(ee-kaw nah-mahn ahng soo-moh-bohk)*

Practice writing. **-Pagsasanay sa pagsulat.** *(pahg-sah-sah-nye sah pahg-soo-laht)*

Good job. **-Magaling.** *(mahg-ah-leeng)*

How do you say _____ in Tagalog?
Paano mo sabihin ang _____ sa Tagalog?
(pah-ah-noh moh sah-bee-heen ahng _____ sah tah-gah-lohg)

Obal *(oh-bahl)* - Oval

Oben *(oh-behn)* - Oven

Obserba *(ohb-sehr-bah)* - Observe

Okey *(oh-key)* - Okay

Oktubre *(ohk-too-breh)* - October

Opiser *(oh-pih-sehr)* - Officer

Opo *(oh-poh)*
Used at the end of a sentence or word as a sign of resepect.
Equivelent to ma'am or sir.

Pp (pah)

I'm going to write the letter P. **-Isusulat ko ang letra P.**
(ee-soo-soo-laht koh ahng lehtra pah)

Trace the letter. **-Bakasin ang letra.** *(bah-kah-seen ahng leh-trah)*

Now you try. **-Ikaw naman ang sumubok.** *(ee-kaw nah-mahn ahng soo-moh-bohk)*

Practice writing. **-Pagsasanay sa pagsulat.** *(pahg-sah-sah-nye sah pahg-soo-laht)*

Good job. **-Magaling.** *(mahg-ah-leeng)*

How do you say _____ in Tagalog?
Paano mo sabihin ang ____ sa Tagalog?
(pah-ah-noh moh sah-bee-heen ahng ____ sah tah-gah-lohg)

Paa *(pah-ah)* - Foot

Paakyat *(pah-ahk-yaht)* - To go up or Climb

Paalam *(pah-ah-lahm)* - Goodbye

Pan *(pahn)* - Bread

Pantalon *(pahn-tah-lohn)* - Pants

Papel *(pah-pehl)* - Paper

Rr (rah)

I'm going to write the letter R. **-Isusulat ko ang letra R.**
(ee-soo-soo-laht koh ahng lehtra rah)

Trace the letter. **-Bakasin ang letra.** *(bah-kah-seen ahng leh-trah)*

Now you try. **-Ikaw naman ang sumubok.** *(ee-kaw nah-mahn ahng soo-moh-bohk)*

Practice writing. **-Pagsasanay sa pagsulat.** *(pahg-sah-sah-nye sah pahg-soo-laht)*

Good job. **-Magaling.** *(mahg-ah-leeng)*

How do you say _____ in Tagalog?
Paano mo sabihin ang _____ sa Tagalog?
(pah-ah-noh moh sah-bee-heen ahng _____ sah tah-gah-lohg)

Radyo *(rah-dyoh)* - Radio

Regalo *(reh-gah-loh)* - Gift

Rosas *(roh-sahs)* - Pink

Reyna *(rey-nah)* - Queen

Relo *(reh-loh)* - Wristwatch

Restoran *(rehs-toh-wrahn)* - Restaurant

Ss (sah)

I'm going to write the letter S. **-Isusulat ko ang letra S.**
(ee-soo-soo-laht koh ahng lehtra sah)

Trace the letter. **-Bakasin ang letra.** *(bah-kah-seen ahng leh-trah)*

Now you try. **-Ikaw naman ang sumubok.** *(ee-kaw nah-mahn ahng soo-moh-bohk)*

Practice writing. **-Pagsasanay sa pagsulat.** *(pahg-sah-sah-nye sah pahg-soo-laht)*

Good job. **-Magaling.** *(mahg-ah-leeng)*

How do you say _____ in Tagalog?
Paano mo sabihin ang ____ sa Tagalog?
(pah-ah-noh moh sah-bee-heen ahng ____ sah tah-gah-lohg)

Sabado *(sah-bah-doh)* - Saturday

Setyembre *(seht-yehm-breh)* - September

Sige na *(see-geh nah)* - Please

Silya *(seel-yah)* - Chair

Sala *(sah-lah)* - Living Room

Sabon *(sah-bohn)* - Soap

Tt (tah)

I'm going to write the letter T. **-Isusulat ko ang letra T.**
(ee-soo-soo-laht koh ahng lehtra tah)

Trace the letter. **-Bakasin ang letra.** *(bah-kah-seen ahng leh-trah)*

Now you try. **-Ikaw naman ang sumubok.** *(ee-kaw nah-mahn ahng soo-moh-bohk)*

Practice writing. **-Pagsasanay sa pagsulat.** *(pahg-sah-sah-nye sah pahg-soo-laht)*

Good job. **-Magaling.** *(mahg-ah-leeng)*

How do you say _____ in Tagalog?
Paano mo sabihin ang ____ sa Tagalog?
(pah-ah-noh moh sah-bee-heen ahng ____ sah tah-gah-lohg)

Tubig *(tooh-big)* - Water

Tinapay *(tee-nah-pye)* - Bread

Tabi-tabi *(tah-bee tah-bee)* - Side by side position

Talong *(tah-lohng)* - Eggplant

Tag-araw *(tahg ahr-raw)* - Summer

Tag-ulan *(tahg ooh-lahn)* - Rainy Season

Uu (ooh)

I'm going to write the letter U. **-Isusulat ko ang letra U.**
(ee-soo-soo-laht koh ahng lehtra ooh)

Trace the letter. **-Bakasin ang letra.** *(bah-kah-seen ahng leh-trah)*

Now you try. **-Ikaw naman ang sumubok.** *(ee-kaw nah-mahn ahng soo-moh-bohk)*

Practice writing. **-Pagsasanay sa pagsulat.** *(pahg-sah-sah-nye sah pahg-soo-laht)*

Good job. **-Magaling.** *(mahg-ah-leeng)*

How do you say _____ in Tagalog?
Paano mo sabihin ang ____ sa Tagalog?
(pah-ah-noh moh sah-bee-heen ahng ____ sah tah-gah-lohg)

Ubas *(ooh-bahs)* - Grapes

Ubo *(ooh-boh)* - Cough

Ulan *(ooh-lahn)* - Rain

Ulap *(ooh-lahp)* - Cloud

Ulo *(ooh-loh)* - Head

Umawit *(ooh-mah-wit)* - To sing

Uwak *(ooh-wahk)* - Crow

Ww (wah)

I'm going to write the letter W. **-Isusulat ko ang letra W.**
(ee-soo-soo-laht koh ahng lehtra wah)

Trace the letter. **-Bakasin ang letra.** (bah-kah-seen ahng leh-trah)

Now you try. **-Ikaw naman ang sumubok.** (ee-kaw nah-mahn ahng soo-moh-bohk)

Practice writing. **-Pagsasanay sa pagsulat.** (pahg-sah-sah-nye sah pahg-soo-laht)

Good job. **-Magaling.** (mahg-ah-leeng)

How do you say _____ in Tagalog?
Paano mo sabihin ang _____ sa Tagalog?
(pah-ah-noh moh sah-bee-heen ahng _____ sah tah-gah-lohg)

Wala (wah-lah) - Nothing

Walang anuman (wah-lahng ah-noo-mahn) - You're welcome

Walumpu (wah-loom-pooh) - Eighty

Yy (yah)

I'm going to write the letter Y. **-Isusulat ko ang letra Y.**
(ee-soo-soo-laht koh ahng lehtra yah)

Trace the letter. **-Bakasin ang letra.** *(bah-kah-seen ahng leh-trah)*

Now you try. **-Ikaw naman ang sumubok.** *(ee-kaw nah-mahn ahng soo-moh-bohk)*

Practice writing. **-Pagsasanay sa pagsulat.** *(pahg-sah-sah-nye sah pahg-soo-laht)*

Good job. **-Magaling.** *(mahg-ah-leeng)*

How do you say _____ in Tagalog?
Paano mo sabihin ang _____ sa Tagalog?
(pah-ah-noh moh sah-bee-heen ahng _____ sah tah-gah-lohg)

Yakap *(yah-kahp)* - Hug

Yelo *(yeh-loh)* - Ice

Yata *(yah-tah)* - Maybe

Yaring-kamay *(yah-reeng-kah-mye)* - Handmade

Yate *(yah-teh)* - Yacht

NAME/PANGALAN

I'm going to write your name. **-Isusulat ko ang pangalan mo.**
(ee-soo-soo-laht koh ahng pah-NGA-lahn moh)

Trace the letters. **-Bakasin ang letra.** *(bah-kah-seen ahng leh-trah)*

Now you try. **-Ikaw naman ang sumubok.** *(ee-kaw nah-mahn ahng soo-moh-bohk)*

Practice writing. **-Pagsasanay sa pagsulat.** *(pahg-sah-sah-nye sah pahg-soo-laht)*

Good job. **-Magaling.** *(mahg-ah-leeng)*

NAME/PANGALAN

I'm going to write your name. **-Isusulat ko ang pangalan mo.**
(ee-soo-soo-laht koh ahng pah-NGA-lahn moh)

Trace the letters. **-Bakasin ang letra.** *(bah-kah-seen ahng leh-trah)*

Now you try. **-Ikaw naman ang sumubok.** *(ee-kaw nah-mahn ahng soo-moh-bohk)*

Practice writing. **-Pagsasanay sa pagsulat.** *(pahg-sah-sah-nye sah pahg-soo-laht)*

Good job. **-Magaling.** *(mahg-ah-leeng)*

LAST NAME/APELYIDO

I'm going to write your last name. **-Isusulat ko ang apelyido mo.**
(ee-soo-soo-laht koh ahng ah-pehl-yee-doh moh)

Trace the letters. **-Bakasin ang letra.** *(bah-kah-seen ahng leh-trah)*

Now you try. **-Ikaw naman ang sumubok.** *(ee-kaw nah-mahn ahng soo-moh-bohk)*

Practice writing. **-Pagsasanay sa pagsulat.** *(pahg-sah-sah-nye sah pahg-soo-laht)*

Good job. **-Magaling.** *(mahg-ah-leeng)*

LAST NAME/APELYIDO

I'm going to write your last name. **-Isusulat ko ang apelyido mo.**
(ee-soo-soo-laht koh ahng ah-pehl-yee-doh moh)

Trace the letters. **-Bakasin ang letra.** *(bah-kah-seen ahng leh-trah)*

Now you try. **-Ikaw naman ang sumubok.** *(ee-kaw nah-mahn ahng soo-moh-bohk)*

Practice writing. **-Pagsasanay sa pagsulat.** *(pahg-sah-sah-nye sah pahg-soo-laht)*

Good job. **-Magaling.** *(mahg-ah-leeng)*

WRITING

Directions:

1) Review the sentence with the student.

2) Help the student write out the sentence.

3) Read it together.

**4) Talk about the phrase by using the prompts
on the left page.**

**Keep in mind that you don't have to be the perfect
linguistic model for your student.**

KEEP TALKING

DON'T OVER CORRECT

LET'S WRITE TOGETHER

Sabay tayong magsulat

sah-bye tah-yohng mahg-soo-laht

WRITING

Let's read and write the sentence. **-Basahin at isulat natin ang pangungusap.**

(bah-sah-heen aht ee-soo-laht nah-teen

ahng pah-NGU-NGU-sahp)

Let me help you write. **-Hayaan mo akong turuan kang magsulat.**

(ha-yah-ahn moh ah-kung tooh-roo-ahn kahng

mahg-soo-laht)

You can trace my letters. **-Maaari mong subaybayan ang aking mga letra.**

(mah-ah-ah-ree mong soo-by-by-yahn ahng

ah-king mung-ah leh-trah)

Make space for each new word. **-Gumawa ng puwang para sa bawat bagong salita.**

(goo-ma-wa nung pooh-wahng pah-rah sah

bah-waht bah-gohng sah-lee-tah)

QUESTIONS TO ASK WHILE YOU'RE WORKING TOGETHER

Do you like school? **-Gusto mo ba eskwela?**

(goo-stoh moh bah es-kweh-lah)

Do you like to study? **-Gusto mo ba magaral?**

(goo-stoh moh bah mahg-ah-rahl)

What is your teacher's name? **-Ano ang pangalan ng iyong guro?**

(ah-noh ahng pahng-ah-lahn nung

ee-yohng gooh-roh)

Do you remember your first day **-Naalala mo ba ang iyong unang araw**

of school? **sa eskwela?**

(nah-ah-lala moh bah ahng ee-yohng oooh-nahng

ah-raow sah ehs-kweh-lah)

I like to go to school.
Gusto kong pumunta sa eskwela.
(gooh-stoh kohng pooh-moon-tah sah ehs-kweh-lah)

WRITING

Let's read and write the sentence.   **-Basahin at isulat natin ang pangungusap.**

(bah-sah-heen aht ee-soo-laht nah-teen

ahng pah-NGU-NGU-sahp)

Let me help you write.   **-Hayaan mo akong turuan kang magsulat.**

(ha-yah-ahn moh ah-kung tooh-roo-ahn kahng

mahg-soo-laht)

You can trace my letters.   **-Maaari mong subaybayan ang aking mga letra.**

(mah-ah-ah-ree mong soo-by-by-yahn ahng

ah-king mung-ah leh-trah)

Make space for each new word   **-Gumawa ng puwang para sa bawat bagong salita.**

(goo-ma-wa nung pooh-wahng pah-rah sah

bah-waht bah-gohng sah-lee-tah)

QUESTIONS TO ASK WHILE YOU'RE WORKING TOGETHER

Do you play soccer?   **-Naglalaro ka ba ng putbol?**

(nahg-lah-lah-roh kah bah nung poot-bohl)

Do you like to bike ride?   **-Gusto mo bang magbisikleta?**

(goo-stoh moh bahng mag-bee-see-kleh-tah)

Do you like running?   **-Gusto mo tumakbo?**

(goo-stoh moh too-mahk-boh)

Can you run on the grass?   **-Maaari ka bang tumakbo sa damuhan?**

(mah-ah-ahree kah bahng too-mahk-boh

sah dah-moo-hahn)

I like to play sports with my friends.
Gusto kong maglaro ng palakasan kasama ang aking mga kaibigan.

(goo-stoh kohng mahg-lah-roh nung pah-lah-kah-sahn kah-sah-mah ahng ah-king mung-ah kye-bee-gahn)

WRITING

Let's read and write the sentence.   **-Basahin at isulat natin ang pangungusap.**

(bah-sah-heen aht ee-soo-laht nah-teen

ahng pah-NGU-NGU-sahp)

Let me help you write.   **-Hayaan mo akong turuan kang magsulat.**

(ha-yah-ahn moh ah-kung tooh-roo-ahn kahng

mahg-soo-laht)

You can trace my letters.   **-Maaari mong subaybayan ang aking mga letra.**

(mah-ah-ah-ree mong soo-by-by-yahn ahng

ah-king mung-ah leh-trah)

Make space for each new word   **-Gumawa ng puwang para sa bawat bagong salita.**

(goo-ma-wa nung pooh-wahng pah-rah sah

bah-waht bah-gohng sah-lee-tah)

QUESTIONS TO ASK WHILE YOU'RE WORKING TOGETHER

What sound do you need to   **-Anong tunog ang kailangan mong marinig**

hear when you have to line   **para pumila sa klase?**

up for class?   *(ah-nohng too-nohg ahng kye-la-NGAN mohng*

mah-ree-neeg pah-rah pooh-mee-lah sah klah-seh)

Is it a bell?   **-Iyon ba ay kampanilya ?**

(ee-yohn bah eye kahm-pah-neel-yah)

A whistle?   **-Sipol?**

(see-pohl)

A teacher?   **-Guru?**

(gooh-roh)

We line up for class.
Pumila tayo sa klase.
(pooh-mee-lah tah-yoh sah klah-seh)

WRITING

Let's read and write the sentence.	**-Basahin at isulat natin ang pangungusap.**
	(bah-sah-heen aht ee-soo-laht nah-teen
	ahng pah-NGU-NGU-sahp)
Let me help you write.	**-Hayaan mo akong turuan kang magsulat.**
	(ha-yah-ahn moh ah-kung tooh-roo-ahn kahng
	mahg-soo-laht)
You can trace my letters.	**-Maaari mong subaybayan ang aking mga letra.**
	(mah-ah-ah-ree mong soo-by-by-yahn ahng
	ah-king mung-ah leh-trah)
Make space for each new word	**-Gumawa ng puwang para sa bawat bagong salita.**
	(goo-ma-wa nung pooh-wahng pah-rah sah
	bah-waht bah-gohng sah-lee-tah)

QUESTIONS TO ASK WHILE YOU'RE WORKING TOGETHER

Who do you sit next to in class?	**-¿Sino ang katabi mong umupo sa klase?**
	(see-noh ahng kah-tah-bee mohng oo-moo-pooh
	sah klah-seh)
The right side or left side?	**-Sa kanan o kaliwa?**
	(sah kah-nahn oh kah-lee-wah)
What are their names?	**-Ano ang kanilang mga pangalan?**
	(ah-noh ahng kah-nee-lahng mung-ah
'	*pah-NGA-lahn)*
Do you help each other?	**-Nagtutulungan ba kayo?**
	(nahg-too-too-loh-NGAN bah kah-yoh)

59

We sit at our table, so we can color and draw.
Nakaupo kami sa aming mesa upang magkulay at gumuhit.

(nah-kah-oo-poh kah-mee sah ah-meeng meh-sah oo-pahng mahg-koo-lie aht goo-moo-hit)

WRITING

Let's read and write the sentence. **-Basahin at isulat natin ang pangungusap.**

(bah-sah-heen aht ee-soo-laht nah-teen

ahng pah-NGU-NGU-sahp)

Let me help you write. **-Hayaan mo akong turuan kang magsulat.**

(ha-yah-ahn moh ah-kung tooh-roo-ahn kahng

mahg-soo-laht)

You can trace my letters. **-Maaari mong subaybayan ang aking mga letra.**

(mah-ah-ah-ree mong soo-by-by-yahn ahng

ah-king mung-ah leh-trah)

Make space for each new word **-Gumawa ng puwang para sa bawat bagong salita.**

(goo-ma-wa nung pooh-wahng pah-rah sah

bah-waht bah-gohng sah-lee-tah)

QUESTIONS TO ASK WHILE YOU'RE WORKING TOGETHER

Do you remember to say, **-Naalala mo bang mag pa salamat?**
"thank you"? *(nah-ah-lah-lah moh bahng mahg pah*

sah-lah-maht)

You can say things like: **-Maaari morin sabihin ang mga bagay tulad ng:**

(ma-ah-ah-ree moh-reen sah-bee-hin ahng

mung-ah bah-guy too-lahd nung)

"Please" **-Pakiusap** *(pah-kee-ooh-sahp)*

"When you're done with that, **-Kapag tapos ka na diyan, maaari ko bang**
may I use it next?" **gamitin ito sa susunod?**

(kah-pahg tah-pohs kah nah dee-yahn,

mah-ah-ah-ree koh bahng gah-mee-tin

ee-toh sah soo-soo-nood)

We share scissors and glue.
Nagbabahagi kami ng gunting at pandikit.

(nahg-bah-bah-hah-gee kah-mee nang goon-teeng aht pahn-dee-kit)

WRITING

Let's read and write the sentence.   **-Basahin at isulat natin ang pangungusap.**

(bah-sah-heen aht ee-soo-laht nah-teen

ahng pah-NGU-NGU-sahp)

Let me help you write.   **-Hayaan mo akong turuan kang magsulat.**

(ha-yah-ahn moh ah-kung tooh-roo-ahn kahng

mahg-soo-laht)

You can trace my letters.   **-Maaari mong subaybayan ang aking mga letra.**

(mah-ah-ah-ree mong soo-by-by-yahn ahng

ah-king mung-ah leh-trah)

Make space for each new word   **-Gumawa ng puwang para sa bawat bagong salita.**

(goo-ma-wa nung pooh-wahng pah-rah sah

bah-waht bah-gohng sah-lee-tah)

QUESTIONS TO ASK WHILE YOU'RE WORKING TOGETHER

How should you sit when   **-Paano ka dapat umupo kapag nasa karpet ka?**

you're on the carpet?   *(pah-ah-noh kah dah-paht oom-oo-poo*

kah-pahg nah-sah kahr-pet kah)

What are your   **-Ano ang mga paborito mong kwento?**

favorite stories?   *(ah-noh ahng mung-ah*

pah-bohr-ee-toh mohng kwehn-toh)

Stories with animals?   **-Kwento sa mga hayop?**

(kwehn-toh sah mung-ah hye-ohp)

We sit on the carpet to listen to stories.
Nakaupo kami sa karpet upang makinig ng mga kwento.

(nah-kaw-oo-poh kah-mee sah kahr-pet oo-pahng mah-kee-nig nang mung-ah kwehn-toh)

WRITING

Let's read and write the sentence. **-Basahin at isulat natin ang pangungusap.**

(bah-sah-heen aht ee-soo-laht nah-teen

ahng pah-NGU-NGU-sahp)

Let me help you write. **-Hayaan mo akong turuan kang magsulat.**

(ha-yah-ahn moh ah-kung tooh-roo-ahn kahng

mahg-soo-laht)

You can trace my letters. **-Maaari mong subaybayan ang aking mga letra.**

(mah-ah-ah-ree mong soo-by-by-yahn ahng

ah-king mung-ah leh-trah)

Make space for each new word **-Gumawa ng puwang para sa bawat bagong salita.**

(goo-ma-wa nung pooh-wahng pah-rah sah

bah-waht bah-gohng sah-lee-tah)

QUESTIONS TO ASK WHILE YOU'RE WORKING TOGETHER

What does your teacher say **-Ano ang sinabi ng iyong guro sa klase para**

for the class to pay attention? **ma bigyan ng pansin?**

(ah-noh ahng see-nah-bee nung ee-yong goo-roh

sah klah-seh pah-rah mah beeg-yahn nung pahn-seen)

"Listen up class." **-Makinig sa klase.**

(mah-kee-neeg sah klah-seh)

"Pay attention." **--Makinig kayo.**

(mah-kee-neeg kai-yoh)

"Quiet, please." **-Tumahimik kayo.**

(tooh-mah-hee-mick kai-yoh)

65

My teacher tells us to be quiet.
Sinabi sa amin ng aking guro
na manahimik kami.

*(see-nah-bee sah ah-meen nung ah-king goo-roh
nah mah-nah-hee-mick kah-mee)*

WRITING

Let's read and write the sentence.   **-Basahin at isulat natin ang pangungusap.**

(bah-sah-heen aht ee-soo-laht nah-teen

ahng pah-NGU-NGU-sahp)

Let me help you write.   **-Hayaan mo akong turuan kang magsulat.**

(ha-yah-ahn moh ah-kung tooh-roo-ahn kahng

mahg-soo-laht)

You can trace my letters.   **-Maaari mong subaybayan ang aking mga letra.**

(mah-ah-ah-ree mong soo-by-by-yahn ahng

ah-king mung-ah leh-trah)

Make space for each new word.   **-Gumawa ng puwang para sa bawat bagong salita.**

(goo-ma-wa nung pooh-wahng pah-rah sah

bah-waht bah-gohng sah-lee-tah)

QUESTIONS TO ASK WHILE YOU'RE WORKING TOGETHER

What songs can you sing?   **-Anong mga kanta ang maaari mong awitin?**

(ah-nohng mung-ah kahn-tah ahng

mah-ah-ahree mohng ah-wee-teen

Let's go on Youtube   **Pumunta tayo sa Youtube at maghanap ng**

and find other songs to sing.   **iba pang mga kantang aawitin.**

(pooh-moon-tah tah-yoh sah Youtube aht

mahg-hahn-ahp nung ee-bah pahng mung-ah

kahn-tahng ah-ah-wee-teen)

Look for: Tong, Tong, Tong

(Crab Song)

We sang songs in class.
Kumanta kami ng mga awitin sa klase.
(koo-mahn-tah kah-mee nang mung-ah ah-wee-teen sah klah-seh)

WRITING

Let's read and write the sentence.   **-Basahin at isulat natin ang pangungusap.**

(bah-sah-heen aht ee-soo-laht nah-teen

ahng pah-NGU-NGU-sahp)

Let me help you write.   **-Hayaan mo akong turuan kang magsulat.**

(ha-yah-ahn moh ah-kung tooh-roo-ahn kahng

mahg-soo-laht)

You can trace my letters.   **-Maaari mong subaybayan ang aking mga letra.**

(mah-ah-ah-ree mong soo-by-by-yahn ahng

ah-king mung-ah leh-trah)

Make space for each new word.   **-Gumawa ng puwang para sa bawat bagong salita.**

(goo-ma-wa nung pooh-wahng pah-rah sah

bah-waht bah-gohng sah-lee-tah)

QUESTIONS TO ASK WHILE YOU'RE WORKING TOGETHER

Do you know how to say the   **-Alam mo ba kung paano sabihin**
Pledge of Allegiance?   **ang pangako ng katapatan?**

(ah-lahm moh bah kung pah-ah-noh sah-bee-hin

ahng pahng-ah-koh nung ka-tah-pah-tahn)

Let's say it together.   **-Sabay nating sabihin.**
English: *(sah-bye nah-teeng sah-bee-hin)*
I pledge allegiance to the flag
of the United States of America,
and to the republic for which
it stands, one nation under God,
indivisible, with liberty and justice
for all.

We recite the Pledge of Allegiance.
Nabigkas namin ang Pangako ng Katapatan.

(nah-beeg-kahs nah-meen ahng
pahng-ah-koh nang kah-tah-pah-tahn)

WRITING

Let's read and write the sentence.-**Basahin at isulat natin ang pangungusap.**

(bah-sah-heen aht ee-soo-laht nah-teen

ahng pah-NGU-NGU-sahp)

Let me help you write.　　　**-Hayaan mo akong turuan kang magsulat.**

(ha-yah-ahn moh ah-kung tooh-roo-ahn kahng

mahg-soo-laht)

You can trace my letters.　　**-Maaari mong subaybayan ang aking mga letra.**

(mah-ah-ah-ree mong soo-by-by-yahn ahng

ah-king mung-ah leh-trah)

Make space for each new word. -**Gumawa ng puwang para sa bawat bagong salita.**

(goo-ma-wa nung pooh-wahng pah-rah sah

bah-waht bah-gohng sah-lee-tah)

QUESTIONS TO ASK WHILE YOU'RE WORKING TOGETHER

Do you have a pet in your class? -**Mayroon ka bang alagang hayop**
　　　　　　　　　　　　　　sa iyong klase?

(may-roh-on kah bahng ah-lah-gahng
hye-ohp sah ee-yohng klah-seh)

What's its name?　　　　　　**-Ano ang pangalan nito?**

(ah-noh ahng pah-NGA-lahn nee-toh)

Do you like it?　　　　　　　**-Gusto mo ba?**

(goo-stoh moh bah)

Does your teacher take it　　　**-Pinalabas ba ito ng iyong guro sa hawla nito?**
out of its cage?　　　　　　　*(pee-nah-lah-bahs bah ee-toh nang ee-yohng*
　　　　　　　　　　　　　　goo-roh sah haow-lah nee-toh)

We have a pet hamster.
Mayroon kaming isang alagang hamster.

(may-roh-on kah-ming ee-sahng ah-lah-gahng hamster)

WRITING

Let's read and write the sentence. **-Basahin at isulat natin ang pangungusap.**

(bah-sah-heen aht ee-soo-laht nah-teen

ahng pah-NGU-NGU-sahp)

Let me help you write. **-Hayaan mo akong turuan kang magsulat.**

(ha-yah-ahn moh ah-kung tooh-roo-ahn kahng

mahg-soo-laht)

You can trace my letters. **-Maaari mong subaybayan ang aking mga letra.**

(mah-ah-ah-ree mong soo-by-by-yahn ahng

ah-king mung-ah leh-trah)

Make space for each new word. **-Gumawa ng puwang para sa bawat bagong salita.**

(goo-ma-wa nung pooh-wahng pah-rah sah

bah-waht bah-gohng sah-lee-tah)

QUESTIONS TO ASK WHILE YOU'RE WORKING TOGETHER

What snacks do you like? **Ano ang gusto mong meryenda?**

(ah-noh ahng goo-stoh mohng mehr-yehn-dah)

Fruit? **-Prutas?** *(prooh-tahs)*

Apples? **-Mansanas?** *(mahn-sah-nahs)*

Yogurt? **-Yogur?** *(yoh-goorr)*

Crackers? **-Biskwit?** *(bees-kweet)*

Do you have something to drink? **-Mayroon ka bang maiinom ?**

(mye-roh-ohn kah bahng mah-ee-ee-nohm)

Is there a water fountain? **-Mayroon bang painuman ng tubig ?**

(mye-roh-ohn bahng pah-ee-noo-mahn nang

too-big)

I like to play.
Gusto kong maglaro.
(gooh-stoh kohng mahg-lah-roh)

WRITING

Let's read and write the sentence. -**Basahin at isulat natin ang pangungusap.**

(bah-sah-heen aht ee-soo-laht nah-teen

ahng pah-NGU-NGU-sahp)

Let me help you write.   -**Hayaan mo akong turuan kang magsulat.**

(ha-yah-ahn moh ah-kung tooh-roo-ahn kahng

mahg-soo-laht)

You can trace my letters.   -**Maaari mong subaybayan ang aking mga letra.**

(mah-ah-ah-ree mong soo-by-by-yahn ahng

ah-king mung-ah leh-trah)

Make space for each new word. -**Gumawa ng puwang para sa bawat bagong salita.**

(goo-ma-wa nung pooh-wahng pah-rah sah

bah-waht bah-gohng sah-lee-tah)

QUESTIONS TO ASK WHILE YOU'RE WORKING TOGETHER

Can you earn points in   -**Maaari ka bang makakuha ng mga puntos sa klase**
class for a prize?   **para sa isang premyo?**

(mah-ah-ah-ree kah bahng mah-kah-koo-hah

nung mung-ah poon-tohs sah klah-seh pah-rah

sah ee-sahng preh-myoh)

What's in the prize box?   -**Ano ang nasa kahon ng premyo?**
(Ah-noh ahng nah-sah kah-hohn nung

preh-myoh)

Toys?   -**Mga laruan.**

(mung-ah lah-roo-ahn)

75

I like to earn points for prizes.
Gusto kong makaipon ng mga puntos para sa premyo.

(goo-stoh kohng mah-kah-ee-pohn nung mung-ah poon-tohs pah-rah sah preh-myoh)

COLOR AND SEARCH

QUESTIONS TO ASK

It looks like he is in the
park riding a bike.

**-Mukhang nasa parke siyang nakasakay
 sa bisikleta.**

*(mook-hahng nah-sah pahr-keh see-yahng
nah-kah-sah-kye sah bee-see-kleh-tah)*

How many kites do you see?

-Ilan saranggola ang nakikita mo?

*(ee-lahn sahr-ahng-gohl-ah ahng
nah-kee-kee-tah mo?)*

Three.

-Tatlo

(taht-loh)

How many dogs are there?

-Ilan ang mga aso doon?

(ee-lahn ahng mung-ah ah-soh doh-ohn)

Two.

-Dalawa.

(dah-lah-wah)

Is this a soccer ball or baseball?

-Ito ba ay isang putbol o baseball?

(ee-toh bah aye ee-sahng poot-bohl oh baseball)

Soccer ball.

-Bolang Pamputbol.

(boh-lahng pahm-poot-bohl)

The Park
Ang pang liwasan
(ahng pahng lee-wah-sahn)

COLOR AND SEARCH

QUESTIONS TO ASK

What is she doing?

-Ano ang ginagawa niya?

(ah-noh ahng gee-nah-gah-wah nee-yah)

Playing with a doll.

-Naglalaro ng isang manika.

(nahg-lah-lah-roh nung ee-sahng mah-nee-kah)

Let's count the number of cars there are on this page.

-Bilangin natin ang bilang ng mga laruang kotse na mayroon sa pahinang ito.

(bee-lah-NGEEN nah-teen ahng bee-lahng nung mung-ah lah-roo-ahng koht-cheh nah mah-eer-roon sah pah-hee-nahng ee-toh)

1 - One

2 - Two

3 - Three

4 - Four

5 - Five

1 - Isa (ee-sah)

2 - Dalawa (dah-lah-wah)

3 - Tatlo (taht-loh)

4 - Apat (ah-paht)

5 - Lima (lee-mah)

How many dolls do you see?

-Ilan ang mga manika na nakikita mo?

(ee-lahn ahng mung-ah mah-nee-kah nah nah-kee-kee-tah moh)

How many teddy bears do you see?

-Ilan ang mga laruan oso na nakikita mo?

(ee-lahn ahng mung-ah lah-roo-ahn oh-soh nah nah-kee-tah moh)

Playtime
Oras ng paglalaro
(oh-rahs nung pahg-lah-lah-roh)

COLOR AND SEARCH

QUESTIONS TO ASK

He is in a library.

-Nasa aklatan siya.

(nah-sah ah-klah-tahn shah)

Point to the globe.
A globe is a model of earth.

-Ituro ang mundo. Ang mundo ay isang modelo ng Daigdig.

(ee-too-roh ahng moon-doh, ahng moon-doh aye ee-sahng moh-deh-loh nung dah-ig-dig)

What kind of shoes is he wearing?
Rain boots.

-Anong klaseng sapatos ang suot niya? Mga bota ng ulan.

(Ah-nohng klah-seng sah-pah-tohs ahng soo-oot nya, mung-ah boh-tah nung oo-lahn)

How many books do you
see on the table?

-Ilan ang mga librong nakikita mo sa mesa?

(ee-lahn ahng mung-ah lee-brong nah-kee-kee-tah moh sah meh-sah)

Four.

-Apat. *(ah-paht)*

How many tables do you see?

-Ilan ang mga mesa na nakikita mo?

(ee-lahn ahng mung-ah meh-sah nah nah-kee-kee-tah moh)

Two.

-Dalawa. *(dah-lah-wah)*

How many chairs?

-Ilan ang upuan?

(ee-lahn ahng oo-pooh-ahn)

Four.

-Apat. *(ah-paht)*

Library
Bahay Aklatan
(bah-hye ah-klah-tahn)

COLOR AND SEARCH

QUESTIONS TO ASK

Point to the tomatoes.

-Ituro ang mga kamatis.

(ee-tooh-roh ahng mung-ah kahm-ah-tees)

How many heads of lettuce do you see?

-Ilan ang mga ulo ng litsugas ang nakikita mo?

(ee-lahn ahng mung-ah ooh-loh nung lit-soo-gahs ahng nah-kee-kee-tah moh)

Two.

-Dalawa. *(dah-lah-wah)*

What is she wearing on her head?

-Ano ang suot niya sa kanyang ulo?

(ah-noh ahng soo-oht nee-yah sah kahn-yahng oo-loh)

A hat.

-Isang sumbrero.

(ee-sahng soom-breh-roh)

Is her cart empty or full?

-Ang kanyang kariton ay walang laman o puno?

(ahng kahn-yahng kah-ree-tohn aye wah-lahng lah-mahn oh pooh-noh)

What else do you see in the picture?

Ano pa ang nakikita mo sa larawan?

(ah-noh pah ahng nah-kee-kee-tah moh sah lah-rah-wahn)

Carrots

-Karot *(kah-roht)*

Broccoli

-Brukoli *(broo-koh-lee)*

Milk

-Gatas *(gah-tahs)*

Butter

-Mantikilya *(mahn-tee-keel-yah)*

Grocery Store
Tindahan ng groceria

(tin-dah-hahn nung gro-seh-ree-ah)

MAZE GAMES

Directions:

1) Cover the Maze Key with your hand.

**2) Allow the student to try
to figure out the puzzle first.**

3) Be encouraging.

**4) Use your prompts to help guide your
student through the maze.**

5) Make it fun!

MAZE GAMES

Let's do a maze after we
complete a page together.

-Gumawa tayo ng isang maze pagkatapos natin
makumpleto nang magkasama ang isang pahina.

(goo-mah-wah tye-oh nung ee-sahng maze
pag-kah-tah-pohs nah-teen mah-koom-pleh-toh nahng
mahg-kah-sah-mah ahng ee-sahng pah-hee-nah)

Want to do a maze together?

-Gusto mo bang gumawa tayo ng maze?

(goo-stoh moh bahng goo-mah-wah tah-yoh nung maze)

Great work today.

-Mahusay na trabaho ngayon.

(ma-hooh-sye nah trah-bah-hoh NGA-yohn)

It'll be a challenge.

-Magiging hamon ito.

(mah-gee-ging hah-mohn ee-toh)

This will be fun.

-Magiging masaya ito!

(mah-gee-ging mah-sye-yah ee-toh)

Very good.

-Napakahusay.

(nah-pah-kah-hoo-sye)

Thank you for trying.

-Salamat sa pagsubok.

(sah-lah-maht sah pahg-soo-bohk)

USE PHRASES THAT ARE APPLICABLE TO YOU

Let's try this maze. **-Subukan natin ang maze na ito.**
(soo-boo-kahn nah-teen ahng maze nah ee-toh)

Start here and find **-Magsimula dito at hanapin ang iyong**
your way out. **daan palabas.**
(mahg-see-moo-lah dee-toh aht hah-nah-peen ahng ee-yohng dah-ahn pah-lah-bahs)

Can I help you? **-Pwede ba kitang matulungan?**
(pweh-deh bah kee-tahng mah-too-loong-ahn)

Turn right. **-Lumiko pakanan**
(loo-mee-koh pah-kahn-nahn)

Turn left. **-Lumiko pakaliwa.**
(loo-me-koh pah-kah-lee-wah)

Down. **-Pababa.**
(pah-bahbah)

Up. **-Pataas.**
(pah-tah-ahs)

Stop there. **-Tumigil ka diyan.** *(too-mee-gihl kah john)*

Oh no! We're stuck. **-Oh hindi! Naligaw tayo.**
(oh heen-dih, nah-lee-gaow tah-yoh)

Try again. **-Subukang muli.**
(soo-boo-kahng moo-lee)

We did it. **-Nagawa natin.**
(nah-gah-wa nah-tin)

ANSWER KEY
Use your hand to shield this Answer Key

Maze 1
Maze Isa
(maze ee-sah)

Start - **Magsimula** *(mahg-see-moo-lah)*

End - **Magtapos** *(mahg-tah-pohs)*

USE PHRASES THAT ARE APPLICABLE TO YOU

Let's try this maze.
-Subukan natin ang maze na ito.
(soo-boo-kahn nah-teen ahng maze nah ee-toh)

Start here and find your way out.
-Magsimula dito at hanapin ang iyong daan palabas.
(mahg-see-moo-lah dee-toh aht hah-nah-peen ahng ee-yohng dah-ahn pah-lah-bahs)

Can I help you?
-Pwede ba kitang matulungan?
(pweh-deh bah kee-tahng mah-too-loong-ahn)

Turn right.
-Lumiko pakanan
(loo-mee-koh pah-kahn-nahn)

Turn left.
-Lumiko pakaliwa.
(loo-me-koh pah-kah-lee-wah)

Down.
-Pababa.
(pah-bahbah)

Up.
-Pataas.
(pah-tah-ahs)

Stop there.
-Tumigil ka diyan. *(too-mee-gihl kah john)*

Oh no! We're stuck.
-Oh hindi! Naligaw tayo.
(oh heen-dih, nah-lee-gaow tah-yoh)

Try again.
-Subukang muli.
(soo-boo-kahng moo-lee)

We did it.
-Nagawa natin.
(nah-gah-wa nah-tin)

ANSWER KEY
Use your hand to shield this Answer Key

Maze 2
Maze Dalawa
(maze dah-lah-wah)

Start -**Magsimula** *(mahg-see-moo-lah)*

End - **Magtapos** *(mahg-tah-pohs)*

USE PHRASES THAT ARE APPLICABLE TO YOU

Let's try this maze.

-Subukan natin ang maze na ito.
(soo-boo-kahn nah-teen ahng maze nah ee-toh)

Start here and find your way out.

-Magsimula dito at hanapin ang iyong daan palabas.
(mahg-see-moo-lah dee-toh aht hah-nah-peen ahng ee-yohng dah-ahn pah-lah-bahs)

Can I help you?

-Pwede ba kitang matulungan?
(pweh-deh bah kee-tahng mah-too-loong-ahn)

Turn right.

-Lumiko pakanan
(loo-mee-koh pah-kahn-nahn)

Turn left.

-Lumiko pakaliwa.
(loo-me-koh pah-kah-lee-wah)

Down.

-Pababa.
(pah-bahbah)

Up.

-Pataas.
(pah-tah-ahs)

Stop there.

-Tumigil ka diyan. *(too-mee-gihl kah john)*

Oh no! We're stuck.

-Oh hindi! Naligaw tayo.
(oh heen-dih, nah-lee-gaow tah-yoh)

Try again.

-Subukang muli.
(soo-boo-kahng moo-lee)

We did it.

-Nagawa natin.
(nah-gah-wa nah-tin)

ANSWER KEY
Use your hand to shield this Answer Key

Maze 3
Maze Tatlo
(maze taht-loh)

Start **-Magsimula** *(mahg-see-moo-lah)*

End **- Magtapos** *(mahg-tah-pohs)*

USE PHRASES THAT ARE APPLICABLE TO YOU

Let's try this maze. **-Subukan natin ang maze na ito.**
(soo-boo-kahn nah-teen ahng maze nah ee-toh)

Start here and find **-Magsimula dito at hanapin ang iyong**
your way out. **daan palabas.**
(mahg-see-moo-lah dee-toh aht hah-nah-peen ahng ee-yohng dah-ahn pah-lah-bahs)

Can I help you? **-Pwede ba kitang matulungan?**
(pweh-deh bah kee-tahng mah-too-loong-ahn)

Turn right. **-Lumiko pakanan**
(loo-mee-koh pah-kahn-nahn)

Turn left. **-Lumiko pakaliwa.**
(loo-me-koh pah-kah-lee-wah)

Down. **-Pababa.**
(pah-bahbah)

Up. **-Pataas.**
(pah-tah-ahs)

Stop there. **-Tumigil ka diyan.** *(too-mee-gihl kah john)*

Oh no! We're stuck. **-Oh hindi! Naligaw tayo.**
(oh heen-dih, nah-lee-gaow tah-yoh)

Try again. **-Subukang muli.**
(soo-boo-kahng moo-lee)

We did it. **-Nagawa natin.**
(nah-gah-wa nah-tin)

ANSWER KEY
Use your hand to shield this Answer Key

Maze 4
Maze Apat
(maze ah-paht)

Start -**Magsimula** *(mahg-see-moo-lah)*

End - **Magtapos** *(mahg-tah-pohs)*

USE PHRASES THAT ARE APPLICABLE TO YOU

Let's try this maze. **-Subukan natin ang maze na ito.**
(soo-boo-kahn nah-teen ahng maze nah ee-toh)

Start here and find your way out. **-Magsimula dito at hanapin ang iyong daan palabas.**
(mahg-see-moo-lah dee-toh aht hah-nah-peen ahng ee-yohng dah-ahn pah-lah-bahs)

Can I help you? **-Pwede ba kitang matulungan?**
(pweh-deh bah kee-tahng mah-too-loong-ahn)

Turn right. **-Lumiko pakanan**
(loo-mee-koh pah-kahn-nahn)

Turn left. **-Lumiko pakaliwa.**
(loo-me-koh pah-kah-lee-wah)

Down. **-Pababa.**
(pah-bahbah)

Up. **-Pataas.**
(pah-tah-ahs)

Stop there. **-Tumigil ka diyan.** *(too-mee-gihl kah john)*

Oh no! We're stuck. **-Oh hindi! Naligaw tayo.**
(oh heen-dih, nah-lee-gaow tah-yoh)

Try again. **-Subukang muli.**
(soo-boo-kahng moo-lee)

We did it. **-Nagawa natin.**
(nah-gah-wa nah-tin)

ANSWER KEY
Use your hand to shield this Answer Key

Maze 5
Maze Lima
(maze lee-mah)

Start -**Magsimula** *(mahg-see-moo-lah)*

End - **Magtapos** *(mahg-tah-pohs)*

USE PHRASES THAT ARE APPLICABLE TO YOU

Let's try this maze. **-Subukan natin ang maze na ito.**
(soo-boo-kahn nah-teen ahng maze nah ee-toh)

Start here and find **-Magsimula dito at hanapin ang iyong**
your way out. **daan palabas.**
(mahg-see-moo-lah dee-toh aht hah-nah-peen ahng ee-yohng dah-ahn pah-lah-bash)

Can I help you? **-Pwede ba kitang matulungan?**
(pweh-deh bah kee-tahng mah-too-loongahn)

Turn right. **-Lumiko pakanan.**
(loo-mee-koh pah-kahn-nahn)

Turn left. **-Lumiko pakaliwa.**
(loo-mee-koh pah-kah-lee-wah)

Down. **-Pababa.**
(pah-bahbah)

Up. **-Pataas.**
(pah-tah-ahs)

Stop there. **-Tumigil ka diyan.** *(too-mee-gihl kah john)*

Oh no! We're stuck. **-Oh hindi! Naligaw tayo.**
(oh heen-dih, nah-lee-gaow tah-yoh)

Try again. **-Subukang muli**
(soo-boo-kahng moo-lee)

We did it. **-Nagawa natin.**
(nah-gah-wa nah-tin)

ANSWER KEY
Use your hand to shield this Answer Key

97

Maze 6
Maze Anim
(maze ah-neem)

Start **-Magsimula** *(mahg-see-moo-lah)*

End - **Magtapos** *(mahg-tah-pohs)*

MAZE GAME 7

USE PHRASES THAT ARE APPLICABLE TO YOU

Let's try this maze.	**-Subukan natin ang maze na ito.** *(soo-boo-kahn nah-teen ahng maze nah ee-toh)*
Start here and find your way out.	**-Magsimula dito at hanapin ang iyong daan palabas.** *(mahg-see-moo-lah dee-toh aht hah-nah-peen ahng ee-yohng dah-ahn pah-lah-bash)*
Can I help you?	**-Pwede ba kitang matulungan?** *(pweh-deh bah kee-tahng mah-too-loongahn)*
Turn right.	**-Lumiko pakanan.** *(loo-mee-koh pah-kahn-nahn)*
Turn left.	-**Lumiko pakaliwa.** *(loo-mee-koh pah-kah-lee-wah)*
Down.	**-Pababa.** *(pah-bahbah)*
Up.	**-Pataas.** *(pah-tah-ahs)*
Stop there.	**-Tumigil ka diyan.** *(too-mee-gihl kah john)*
Oh no! We're stuck.	**-Oh hindi! Naligaw tayo.** *(oh heen-dih, nah-lee-gaow tah-yoh)*
Try again.	**-Subukang muli** *(soo-boo-kahng moo-lee)*
We did it.	**-Nagawa natin.** *(nah-gah-wa nah-tin)*

ANSWER KEY
Use your hand to shield the this Answer Key

Maze 7
Maze Pito
(maze pee-toh)

Start **-Magsimula** *(mahg-see-moo-lah)*

End - **Magtapos** *(mahg-tah-pohs)*

MAZE GAME 8

USE PHRASES THAT ARE APPLICABLE TO YOU

Let's try this maze.	**-Subukan natin ang maze na ito.** *(soo-boo-kahn nah-teen ahng maze nah ee-toh)*
Start here and find your way out.	**-Magsimula dito at hanapin ang iyong daan palabas.** *(mahg-see-moo-lah dee-toh aht hah-nah-peen ahng ee-yohng dah-ahn pah-lah-bash)*
Can I help you?	**-Pwede ba kitang matulungan?** *(pweh-deh bah kee-tahng mah-too-loongahn)*
Turn right.	**-Lumiko pakanan.** *(loo-mee-koh pah-kahn-nahn)*
Turn left.	**-Lumiko pakaliwa.** *(loo-mee-koh pah-kah-lee-wah)*
Down.	**-Pababa.** *(pah-bahbah)*
Up.	**-Pataas.** *(pah-tah-ahs)*
Stop there.	**-Tumigil ka diyan.** *(too-mee-gihl kah john)*
Oh no! We're stuck.	**-Oh hindi! Naligaw tayo.** *(oh heen-dih, nah-lee-gaow tah-yoh)*
Try again.	**-Subukang muli** *(soo-boo-kahng moo-lee)*
We did it.	**-Nagawa natin.** *(nah-gah-wa nah-tin)*

ANSWER KEY
Use your hand to shield the this Answer Key

Maze 8
Maze Walo
(maze wah-loh)

Start -**Magsimula** *(mahg-see-moo-lah)*

End - **Magtapos** *(mahg-tah-pohs)*

USE PHRASES THAT ARE APPLICABLE TO YOU

Let's try this maze.	**-Subukan natin ang maze na ito.** *(soo-boo-kahn nah-teen ahng maze nah ee-toh)*
Start here and find your way out.	**-Magsimula dito at hanapin ang iyong daan palabas.** *(mahg-see-moo-lah dee-toh aht hah-nah-peen ahng ee-yohng dah-ahn pah-lah-bash)*
Can I help you?	**-Pwede ba kitang matulungan?** *(pweh-deh bah kee-tahng mah-too-loongahn)*
Turn right.	**-Lumiko pakanan.** *(loo-mee-koh pah-kahn-nahn)*
Turn left.	**-Lumiko pakaliwa.** *(loo-mee-koh pah-kah-lee-wah)*
Down.	**-Pababa.** *(pah-bahbah)*
Up.	**-Pataas.** *(pah-tah-ahs)*
Stop there.	**-Tumigil ka diyan.** *(too-mee-gihl kah john)*
Oh no! We're stuck.	**-Oh hindi! Naligaw tayo.** *(oh heen-dih, nah-lee-gaow tah-yoh)*
Try again.	**-Subukang muli** *(soo-boo-kahng moo-lee)*
We did it.	**-Nagawa natin.** *(nah-gah-wa nah-tin)*

ANSWER KEY
Use your hand to shield the this Answer Key

Maze 9
Maze Siyam
(maze shyahm)

Start -**Magsimula** *(mahg-see-moo-lah)*

End - **Magtapos** *(mahg-tah-pohs)*

MAZE GAME 10

<u>USE PHRASES THAT ARE APPLICABLE TO YOU</u>

Let's try this maze.
-Subukan natin ang maze na ito.
(soo-boo-kahn nah-teen ahng maze nah ee-toh)

Start here and find your way out.
-Magsimula dito at hanapin ang iyong daan palabas.
(mahg-see-moo-lah dee-toh aht hah-nah-peen ahng ee-yohng dah-ahn pah-lah-bash)

Can I help you?
-Pwede ba kitang matulungan?
(pweh-deh bah kee-tahng mah-too-loongahn)

Turn right.
-Lumiko pakanan.
(loo-mee-koh pah-kahn-nahn)

Turn left.
-Lumiko pakaliwa.
(loo-mee-koh pah-kah-lee-wah)

Down.
-Pababa.
(pah-bahbah)

Up.
-Pataas.
(pah-tah-ahs)

Stop there.
-Tumigil ka diyan. *(too-mee-gihl kah john)*

Oh no! We're lost.
-Oh hindi! Naligaw tayo.
(oh heen-dih, nah-lee-gaow tah-yoh)

Try again.
-Subukang muli
(soo-boo-kahng moo-lee)

We did it.
-Nagawa natin.
(nah-gah-wa nah-tin)

ANSWER KEY
Use your hand to shield the this Answer Key

105

Maze 10
Maze Sampu
(maze sahm-pooh)

Start **-Magsimula** *(mahg-see-moo-lah)*

End **- Magtapos** *(mahg-tah-pohs)*

STUDENT PHRASES

Yes -**Oo.**
(oh-oh)

No -**Hindi.**
(heen-dih)

I don't know. -**Hindi ko alam.**
(heen-dih koh ah-lahm)

I don't understand. -**Hindi ko maintindihan.**
(heen-dih koh mah-een-teen-dee-hahn)

Can you help me? -**Maaari mo ba akong tulungan.**
(mah-ah-ah-ree moh bah ah-kohng too-loo-NGAN)

How do you say _____ -**Paano mo sasabihin _____ ?**
(pah-ah-noh moh sah-sah-bee-heen)

Thank you. -**Salamat** *(sah-lah-maht)*

I'm learning to speak Tagalog.
Natututo akong magsalita ng tagalog.
(nah-too-too-toh ah-kohng mahg-sah-lee-tah nung tah-gah-lohg)

This is fun. -**Ito ay masaya**
(ee-toh eye mah-sah-yah)

Can we do a Maze?
Maaari ba tayong gumawa ng isang maze?
(mah-ah-ahree bah tah-yong goo-mah-wah nung ee-sahng maze)

Let me try. -**Hayaan mo akong subukan.**
(hah-yah-ahn moh ah-kong soo-boo-kahn)

High Frequency Words

ako	I	**ano**	what
ikaw, ka	you	**alin**	which
siya	he / she	**saan**	where
kami	we (excluding the listener)	**nasaan**	where
tayo	we (we + you)	**ito**	this
kayo	you / you all	**at**	and
sila	they	**sino**	who
akin	my / mine	**dahil**	because
iyo	your	**laro**	play
kanya	his/her	**kinig**	listen
inyo, ninyo	your	**naku**	oh! or oh no!
kanila	their	**sa**	at

CPSIA information can be obtained
at www.ICGtesting.com
Printed in the USA
LVHW061255040122
707823LV00016B/153